RUBANK EDUCATIONAL LIBRARY No. 139

CLASSICAL STUDIES

Based
Upon
the
Solo
Sonatas,
Partitas,
and
Suites,
of
Bach
and
Handel

for
CLARINET
TRANSCRIBED AND EDITED
by
H. VOXMAN

RUBANK®

HAL•LEONARD®
CORPORATION
7777 W. BLUEMOUND RD. P.O. BOX 13819 MILWAUKEE, WI 53213

PREFACE

*T*HE works of Johann Sebastian Bach (1685-1750) for un-accompanied violin and unaccompanied cello, are universally acknowledged to be among the greatest in the heritage of masterworks handed down by this illustrious master of the art of music. Widespread use of these compositions over a period of nearly a hundred years has proved that they are almost indispensable in the teaching and performing reper-toires of the instruments for which they were written. A first hand acquaintanceship through actual performance of such works, musically sufficient in themselves without the aid or support of other instruments, is a highly desirable experience for all modern instrumentalists.

It is highly fortunate that transcriptions of these works for clarinet present no great difficulties; neither do they contain offending compromises. For the most part, they accommo-date the range and character of the instrument admirably, and afford the serious student a wealth of fine music well-suited to the study of phrasing and articulation.

The partitas and suites, written in what apparently are dance rhythms, are constructed in reality of musical forms which for the most part had ceased to be dances long before Bach utilized them as vehicles for some of his most elaborate writing. The skillful employment of themes in these tradi-tional forms, however, offers scope for the greatest ingenuity on the part of the composer; likewise, it provides opportunity for unlimited possibilities in the development of musicianship on the part of the performer.

To the transcriptions of the unaccompanied sonatas, partitas, and suites, presented on the following pages, a number of choice extracts have been added from various keyboard compositions of both Bach and his great contemporary, George Frideric Handel (1685-1759). This additional ma-terial will prove valuable as a means to enhance further the study of the classical form and style.

H. Voxman

Historical Comments and Interpretative Notes

*B*ACH'S unaccompanied sonatas, partitas, and suites were composed during his appointment as Kapellmeister to the princely *Court at Cöthen* (1717-1723). These works were not known, in general, to his contemporaries. It was not until almost a century after Bach's death that Felix Mendelssohn-Bartholdy (1809-1847), and his côterie of musical enthusiasts, most effectively called attention to the fact that Bach, a then inadequately-known genius, had left to humanity a wealth of great music which was a veritable treasure of unexplored beauty.

In particular, credit must go to Ferdinand David (1810-1873), a professor in Mendelssohn's famed *Leipzig Conservatory*, for having brought from obscurity the solo sonatas and par-titas, thus earning the undying gratitude of the musical world. It was David who first edited and published them before they were accepted at large. He also influenced his close friend, the immortal violinist Joseph Joachim (1831-1907), to per-form the works throughout the world, thereby giving them the widespread hearing they so deserved.

In our own time, the renowned Spanish cellist, Pablo Casals (1876-1973), has established himself as the greatest of mod-ern interpreters of the solo suites. Students are strongly urged to study his performances, which have been recorded by H.M.V. for the *Bach Society* (England). Various excel-lent recordings of the solo sonatas for violin are listed in domestic and foreign catalogs as well. Today, the interpre-tative study of these masterworks is a fundamental pillar in the field of musical scholarship.

★ ★ ★

*I*N performing the music of Bach, observe that the phrase generally does not end with the bar-line. This characteristic of Bach's writing must be borne in mind, particularly when breath is to be taken. In addition, trills should begin with the upper accessory.

Trills in figures such as:

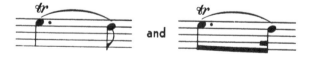

are executed in the manner of:

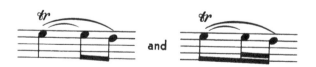

When performing works of this period, the tradition is to retard the end of a strain upon its repetition.

CONTENTS

Studies from the Works for Solo Violin by Bach

Studies from the Works for Solo Cello by Bach

Studies from Other Works by Bach and Handel

PRESTO

Sonata I in G Minor

Bach

ALLEMANDE
Partita I in B Minor

Bach

DOUBLE
Partita I in B Minor

Bach

CORRENTE
Partita I in B Minor

Bach

DOUBLE

Partita I in B Minor

Bach

DOUBLE
Partita I in B Minor

Bach

BOURRÉE

Partita I in B Minor

Bach

DOUBLE

Partita I in B Minor

Bach

Allegro (♩ = 92)

II^{da} volta riten.

ALLEGRO
Sonata II in A Minor

Bach

ALLEMANDE
Partita II in D Minor

Bach

(♩ = 76) (not too detached)

IIda. volta rit.

1033-71

GIGUE
Partita II in D Minor

Bach

COURANTE

Partita II in D Minor

Bach

II.^{da} volta rit.

ALLEGRO ASSAI
Sonata III in C Major

Bach

1033-71

GAVOTTE EN RONDO

Partita III in E Major

Bach

BOURRÉE

Partita III in E Major

Bach

GIGUE

Partita III in E Major

Bach

II^da volta rit.

1033-71

PRÉLUDE

Suite I

Allegro moderato (♩=96)

Bach

ALLEMANDE

Suite I

Bach

Moderato, con grandezza (♩ = 72)

COURANTE
Suite I

Bach

Allegro non troppo ($\quarternote = 104$)

SARABANDE

Suite I

Bach

MINUETS

Suite I

Bach

II

GIGUE

Suite I

Bach

PRÉLUDE

Suite II

Allegro moderato (♩ = 88)

Bach

ALLEMANDE
Suite II

Bach

COURANTE
Suite II

Bach

SARABANDE
Suite II

Bach

Lento (♩ = 60)

MINUETS
Suite II

Bach

GIGUE
Suite II

Bach

Allegro (♩. = 69)

ALLEMANDE

Suite III

Bach

Moderato (♪ = 112)

PRÉLUDE

Suite III

Bach

Allegro (♩ = 88)

SARABANDE
Suite III

Bach

Lento (♪ =66)

BOURRÉES
Suite III

I

Bach

II

Bourrée I D.C.

COURANTE
Suite III

Allegro (♩ = 144)

Bach

GIGUE
Suite III

Bach

PRELUDE
Suite IV

Bach

ALLEMANDE
Suite IV

Bach

COURANTE
Suite IV

Bach

SARABANDE
Suite IV

Bach

1033-71

BOURRÉES
Suite IV
I

Bach

Fine *mf*

p cresc.

cresc.

‖

p-pp   *mf*   *cresc.*

Bourrée I D.C.

GIGUE
Suite IV

Bach

IIda volta rall.

PRÉLUDE
Suite VI

Bach

61

1033-71

COURANTE
Suite VI

Allegro non troppo (♩ = 112)

Bach

GIGUE

Suite VI

Bach

MODERATO

Second Little Prelude

Bach

ALLEGRO
Suite II

Allegro

Handel

ALLEGRO
Suite X

Allegro

Handel

GIGUE
Suite XIV

Presto

Handel

ALLEGRO
Sonata in E Major

Bach

(1) In this movement interpret all grace notes ♪ as ♪.

SARABANDE

Partita in B♭

Bach